The No-Nonsense Job Search & Career Playbook

Lee Harding

Copyright © 2024 Lee Harding

All rights reserved.

ISBN: 9798338957707

CONTENTS

1. Introduction: The New World of Work — 1
2. Job Search Mindset 2.0 — 2
3. Personal Branding: Your Career Story — 4
4. Networking Like a Pro — 9
5. Optimizing Your LinkedIn Profile — 13
6. Mastering the Gig Economy & Freelance Work — 17
7. The Hidden Job Market — 21
8. Writing Your CV for Different Stages and Industries — 25
9. Advanced LinkedIn Techniques — 29
10. Preparing for Every Type of Interview — 32
11. Salary Negotiation Masterclass — 36
12. After the Offer: Navigating Your First 90 Days — 38
13. Career Growth and Development — 40
14. Career Pivots & Returning to Work After a Break — 43
15. Navigating Toxic Work Environments & Knowing When to Leave — 45
16. Job Searching in a Global Market — 47
17. Final Thoughts: Your Career, Your Journey — 49

INTRODUCTION:
THE NEW WORLD OF WORK

Searching for a job is hard. There's no sugar-coating it, and I'm not going to start now. Whether you've got a job and are thinking of moving on, or you're out of work and hustling hard for the next opportunity, searching for a job is tough. I've seen it time and time again throughout my 20+ years in recruitment, and while the methods for job searching might have changed, the challenges are as real as ever.

Today's job market is an unpredictable beast. With the rise of remote work, gig economies, and global hiring, opportunities are everywhere—but they're also harder to grab. You're not just competing with the guy down the street anymore; you're up against candidates from around the world.

If you're like most people, you're overwhelmed by conflicting advice on CVs, interviews, job applications, and recruiters. Some "gurus" want you to believe there's a magical formula for landing a job, but here's the truth: there's no one-size-fits-all solution. There are, however, a set of tried-and-true strategies that can work for anyone, in any industry.

That's where this guide comes in. I've worked for recruitment agencies, built internal recruitment teams from scratch, and consulted for some of the biggest companies in the world. What you'll get in this guide is not fluff—it's the real deal. I'm going to walk you through the entire job search process, cut through the BS, and give you actionable tips that will help you land the job you want.

Whether you're just starting your career or you're looking for a change after decades in the workforce, this guide will give you the tools you need to make your job search easier, faster, and far less painful.

So, let's get into it.

CHAPTER 1:
JOB SEARCH MINDSET 2.0

Before you start pounding the pavement (or, more likely, scrolling through job boards at 2 a.m.), you need to get your mindset right. A lot of people jump straight into writing their CV without taking a moment to really think about why they want a new job and what they hope to get out of it.

Why are you really looking for a new job?

Maybe it's because you're stuck in a rut, or you've had it up to here with your current boss. Maybe you want more money, better work-life balance, or a chance to chase something new and exciting. Or, maybe you're simply in a position where you need a paycheck—like, yesterday. Whatever it is, you need to define your "why" before you even start searching.

Taking Stock of Your "Why"

It's easy to say "I just want a better job," but what does that actually mean? Here's the exercise I recommend: Sit down with a pen and paper, and make two lists. On the first list, write down all the reasons you're looking for a new job. On the second list, outline what you want from your next role. Be as specific as possible.

For example, if you're chasing a higher salary, what number are you aiming for? If you want more of a challenge, what does that look like? Does "better work-life balance" mean flexible hours, the ability to work from home, or fewer late nights? Write it all down, and don't worry if it feels like a wish list right now.

Once you've written your lists, go back and highlight your non-negotiables. These are the things you absolutely cannot compromise on. The rest? They're nice-to-haves but not deal-breakers. This process helps you zero in on the kinds of roles that are worth your time and energy to pursue.

Managing Expectations

Here's the reality: your next job isn't going to solve all of your problems. Sorry, but it's true. A better salary might ease financial stress, but it won't magically make your workday feel shorter. A less toxic boss doesn't mean you'll never have to deal with office politics. The grass isn't always greener, and sometimes, it's just a different shade of the same old green.

That said, having clear goals and realistic expectations sets you up for success. If you go into your job search with a solid understanding of what you want—and what you're willing to accept—you'll be less likely to waste time on roles that aren't a good fit.

Building Resilience

Let's get one thing straight: you're going to get rejected. It's not a matter of if, but when. And that's okay. The key is to build resilience so you don't lose momentum after a few setbacks. Rejection is part of the game, but it doesn't define your value as a candidate.

Here are a few ways to keep your head in the game during a long job search:

- **Set Small, Achievable Goals:** Instead of focusing solely on landing the job, break your job search into smaller steps. Submit 5 quality applications a week, or send 3 networking messages a day. Celebrate these mini-wins to keep your motivation high.

- **Take Breaks:** Job hunting can be exhausting. If you're feeling burnt out, take a day or two off from it. The jobs will still be there when you get back.

- **Stay Positive:** Easier said than done, I know. But staying positive isn't about pretending everything's perfect—it's about focusing on the things you can control, like how prepared you are for interviews or how you present yourself in your CV.

A clear mindset is the foundation of a successful job search. By understanding your "why," managing your expectations, and building resilience, you'll be equipped to handle the ups and downs of your job search journey. Take your time to reflect on your career goals, stay focused, and remember that finding the right job is a marathon, not a sprint

CHAPTER 2:

PERSONAL BRANDING—YOUR CAREER STORY

In today's job market, you need to be more than just a job seeker—you need to be a **brand**. Personal branding isn't just for influencers or entrepreneurs; it's for anyone who wants to stand out in their industry and communicate what they offer in a compelling, authentic way.

What is Personal Branding?

Your personal brand is the story you tell the world about who you are, what you do, and what makes you different. It's how you present yourself online, on paper, and in person. Whether you realize it or not, you already have a personal brand. Now it's time to take control of it and make it work for you in your job search.

Think of your personal brand as the sum of your:

- **Professional experience:** Your career history, achievements, and the skills you've developed.
- **Values and strengths:** What drives you? What do you do better than anyone else?
- **Unique traits:** What makes you different from others in your field? This could be your approach to problem-solving, a skill set that sets you apart, or your ability to lead in a specific context.

You want to build a cohesive story around these elements. Your goal is to present a clear, consistent picture of who you are, so that when recruiters, employers, or potential connections see your CV, LinkedIn profile, or portfolio, they know exactly what you bring to the table.

Crafting Your Career Story

Your personal brand is really about shaping how people perceive you. To do this effectively, you need to craft a career story that not only highlights your skills but also aligns with your career goals.

Here's how to start:

1. Define Your Unique Selling Proposition (USP)

What sets you apart from the crowd? Are you the "data-driven marketing expert"? The "operations leader with a passion for streamlining processes"?

Your USP should be clear, concise, and specific enough that it makes people think of you when they hear about roles in your field.

2. Create a Narrative

Look at your career as a story with a beginning, middle, and end.

Instead of viewing your work experience as a list of jobs, think about how each role has contributed to your growth and what themes emerge.

For example, maybe every job you've had involves transforming underperforming teams into high-functioning ones. That's a story you can tell across all your branding materials.

Your story should answer these questions:

- How did you get started in your career?
- What are the major milestones you've achieved along the way?
- What skills have you developed and what impact have you made?
- Where are you headed next, and why?

3. Align Your Brand with Your Career Goals

Make sure that the brand you're building today aligns with where you want to go in the future.

If you're pivoting into a new industry or role, you need to reframe your experience in a way that speaks to your new direction.

Highlight transferable skills, projects, or roles that show your qualifications for your next step.

Your Branding Toolkit

Once you've defined your personal brand, it's time to put it to work. There are three primary tools you'll use to communicate your brand: your CV, your LinkedIn profile, and your personal website or portfolio.

Your CV:

Your CV is often the first thing a recruiter will see, so it needs to clearly communicate your career story.

This is where you emphasize the skills, achievements, and roles that align with the job you're applying for. (More on this in Chapter 7: Writing a CV that Stands Out.)

LinkedIn Profile:

Your LinkedIn profile is your public-facing brand. This is where you showcase not only your work history but also your professional interests and personality. (I'll dig deeper into optimizing LinkedIn in Chapter 4.)

Personal Website or Portfolio:

If you're in a field where visual or project-based work is important (like design, writing, or tech), you need a website or portfolio to showcase your best work.

But even if your work isn't project-based, a personal website can help you highlight your career story, share testimonials, or publish articles about your industry, which positions you as an expert.

Online Presence: Beyond LinkedIn

Your personal brand extends beyond LinkedIn. Employers and recruiters may also check out your other social media profiles or Google your name. Here's how to make sure your online presence aligns with your professional brand:

- **Twitter/X:** If you're active on Twitter, use it to share industry insights, follow thought leaders, and engage with relevant conversations. Just make sure your profile reflects your personal brand. Keep personal opinions and controversial posts in check.

- **Instagram or Personal Blog:** If you're in a creative field, Instagram or a personal blog can be great places to showcase your work or ideas. For example, UX designers, photographers, and writers can use these platforms to build a following and demonstrate their skills.

- **Facebook:** Even if you don't use Facebook for work, keep your privacy settings in mind. Employers may still search for your profile, so make sure that anything public aligns with the brand you want to convey.

- **YouTube:** Some professionals use YouTube to share tutorials, industry commentary, or case studies. If you're comfortable on video, this can be a powerful way to grow your personal brand.

Maintaining Consistency Across Platforms

Your personal brand should be consistent across all platforms. That doesn't mean you have to repeat the same things on every site, but your messaging, tone, and core narrative should align.

If your CV highlights your expertise in project management but your LinkedIn profile looks like it belongs to a generalist without focus, you're sending mixed signals.

Take a moment to audit your online presence:

- Does your CV align with your LinkedIn profile?
- Do your social media profiles (including Twitter, Instagram, etc.) present a consistent professional image?
- Are there any old accounts or posts that don't reflect who you are now or where you're going? Clean those up.

Building Thought Leadership

One of the best ways to establish a personal brand is to position yourself as a thought leader in your field. Thought leadership isn't just for C-level execs—it's about showing that you're knowledgeable, passionate, and ahead of the curve in your industry.

Here's how to get started:

1. **Share Insights on LinkedIn:** Start by sharing articles, insights, or your thoughts on industry trends. You don't need

to be a prolific writer—just focus on quality, not quantity.

2. **Start a Blog or Publish Articles:** If you enjoy writing, consider starting a blog where you can share longer-form content. This helps build credibility and shows potential employers that you're deeply engaged in your field. If a blog seems like too much work, LinkedIn's publishing platform is a great place to post articles.

3. **Speak at Industry Events or Webinars:** Look for opportunities to speak at industry events, conferences, or even webinars. This can be a great way to network and grow your brand's visibility.

4. **Join Podcasts or Create Your Own:** Podcasts are a growing medium, and if you're comfortable speaking, they can be a great way to showcase your expertise. You could either be a guest on existing podcasts or, if you're ambitious, start your own.

Final Thought: Be Authentic

At the end of the day, your personal brand should feel authentic. You don't want to create a persona that's impossible to maintain. The key to a strong personal brand is being clear about who you are, where you're going, and how your unique experience and skills set you apart.

When you're authentic, people will be drawn to your story—and that's how you create opportunities

CHAPTER 3:
NETWORKING LIKE A PRO

Most people dread the idea of networking. It's awkward, uncomfortable, and can feel like forced small talk—but if you want to open doors in your career, you're going to need to network. Here's the thing: networking is not about schmoozing or showing off. It's about building genuine relationships that can lead to opportunities down the road.

Why Networking Matters

You've probably heard that 70% of jobs aren't advertised. While that might be a slight exaggeration, the reality is that many roles are filled through internal referrals, word of mouth, or connections. This is the hidden job market—positions that aren't listed on job boards or company websites. If you're not networking, you're missing out on those unlisted opportunities.

Think of networking as planting seeds. You might not get immediate results, but over time, those relationships can grow into something valuable—whether it's a job lead, a new connection, or even a mentor.

Networking isn't just about finding jobs. It's also about learning from others, staying up-to-date with industry trends, and creating a professional support system. It's an ongoing process that, when done well, can open doors you didn't even know existed.

Online Networking: Leveraging LinkedIn

Networking has moved online in a big way, especially since remote work and virtual meetings have become the norm. That's where LinkedIn comes into play.

If you're not using LinkedIn effectively, you're leaving opportunities on the table.

Here's how you can up your LinkedIn game and network like a pro:

1. Optimize Your LinkedIn Profile
Your LinkedIn profile is essentially your digital business card. It's often the first impression people will have of you, so you need to make sure it's polished and aligned with your personal brand. (Check out Chapter 4 for a deep dive on optimizing your profile.)

2. Engage with Content Regularly
Don't be a LinkedIn lurker. If you're not active, people will assume you're not looking for opportunities or that you're not serious about your career. Aim to comment on posts, share articles, and engage with content related to your industry at least a few times a week.

When you comment on posts, add value. Instead of a generic "Great post!" reply, offer an insight or ask a question. This sparks conversations and helps you stand out from the sea of comments.

3. Personalize Your Connection Requests
It's easy to hit "Connect" and hope for the best, but that's not networking—it's collecting. When you send a connection request, take a moment to add a personalized note. Something as simple as this works:

"Hi [Name], I saw your recent post on [topic] and found it really insightful. I'd love to connect and hear more about your work in [field]."

This shows that you're genuinely interested in the person and not just randomly adding people to your network.

4. Use LinkedIn Groups
LinkedIn groups are a goldmine for meeting like-minded professionals. Find groups related to your industry or areas of interest, and participate in discussions. It's a great way to get noticed without feeling like you're directly "networking." Plus, many people post job openings or opportunities within these groups that aren't listed elsewhere.

5. Reach Out for Informational Interviews
Don't wait until you're actively job hunting to reach out to people. If there's someone whose career path you admire or who works at a company you're interested in, ask for an informational interview. This is a low-pressure way to network and gather valuable insights about a company, industry, or role.

Here's a simple message you can send on LinkedIn:

"Hi [Name], I've been following your work at [Company] and really admire what you've accomplished in [industry]. I'm interested in learning more about [field] and would love to hear about your experience over a quick 15-minute call if you're open to it."

In-Person Networking

Online networking is great, but in-person events are still incredibly valuable. Whether it's industry conferences, local meetups, or casual coffee chats, face-to-face interactions can make a lasting impression.

1. Be Prepared
Before any event, do a little homework. Find out who's going to be there, what companies will be represented, and who you might want to talk to. Have a few talking points or questions ready, so you're not scrambling to make conversation.

2. Focus on Asking Questions
People love to talk about themselves. If you're feeling awkward or unsure how to start a conversation, just ask a question. Something like, "How did you get into [industry]?" or "What do you think of [event topic] so far?" can easily kick off a meaningful conversation.

3. Have a Quick Pitch Ready
You don't need to deliver a rehearsed speech, but you should have a clear, concise answer to the inevitable "So, what do you do?" question. Think of it as your elevator pitch. Aim for something short and to the point, like:

"I'm a project manager in the tech industry, focusing on improving workflow efficiencies for remote teams."

4. Follow Up
After meeting someone, don't just disappear. Send a follow-up message on LinkedIn or via email within a few days. Mention something specific from your conversation to jog their memory and continue the relationship from there. Here's a quick example:

"Hi [Name], it was great meeting you at [event]! I really enjoyed our chat about [topic]. Let's stay in touch, and I'd love to continue the conversation."

The Power of Weak Ties

One of the biggest networking mistakes people make is focusing only on close connections—people they already know well. But studies show that weak ties, or more distant acquaintances, are often more powerful when it comes to finding job opportunities.

Why? Because your close connections are likely tapped into the same opportunities as you. It's the people on the fringes of your network—old colleagues, distant acquaintances, people you've only interacted with online—that can introduce you to new, unexpected opportunities.

So don't be afraid to reach out to people you haven't spoken to in a while. A simple "I'd love to catch up and see what you've been working on!" message can re-establish the connection and potentially lead to new opportunities.

Networking When You're Introverted

Not everyone enjoys the idea of networking, especially if you're introverted. The good news? Networking doesn't have to be a high-energy, extroverted activity. In fact, introverts can be great at networking because they tend to build deeper, more meaningful connections.

Here are a few tips for introverts:

- Start small: Focus on building a few meaningful connections instead of trying to meet everyone at an event.

- Leverage online networking: Introverts often thrive in written communication, so lean into LinkedIn or email if that feels more comfortable than in-person networking.

- Prepare talking points: Having a few conversation starters ready can make networking less intimidating.

Networking isn't about collecting business cards or making small talk—it's about building meaningful relationships. By nurturing your network, both online and in person, you'll tap into opportunities that may never reach the public eye.

Whether you're actively job hunting or just staying open to new possibilities, consistent networking can become your secret weapon in the job market

CHAPTER 4:
OPTIMIZING YOUR LINKEDIN PROFILE

Let's face it: LinkedIn is the recruiter's playground. If you're not on LinkedIn, or if your profile isn't optimized, you're making it harder for recruiters to find you. It's not just about having a profile—it's about using it strategically to showcase your skills, experience, and personal brand.

Your LinkedIn Profile: Your Digital Resume and Portfolio

Think of your LinkedIn profile as your personal website. It's your chance to show the world what you do, what you've accomplished, and what you bring to the table.

While your CV might be tailored to specific jobs, your LinkedIn profile should showcase the full picture of who you are as a professional.

1. Profile Picture: First Impressions Matter

Your profile picture is the first thing people see when they come across your LinkedIn page. This isn't the place for selfies or casual photos. You don't need a professional photographer, but your picture should be clear, professional, and friendly.

Pro tip: A smiling, approachable profile picture tends to attract more connections and engagement.

2. Headline: Your 10-Second Pitch

Your headline is prime real estate—it's the second thing people see after your picture. Many people make the mistake of only listing their job title here, but you can do so much more. Use this space to showcase your value and stand out.

Instead of just saying "Project Manager," try something like: "Project Manager | Expert in Agile Methodologies | Helping Teams Deliver Results Faster."

3. About Section: Your Career Story

This is where you can go beyond your job titles and tell your career story. It's your chance to highlight your skills, achievements, and personality. Don't just list your roles—talk about what motivates you and what sets you apart.

Example:

"I'm a seasoned project manager with a passion for leading cross-functional teams to deliver complex projects. With over 10 years of experience in the tech industry, I specialize in improving workflows, enhancing team collaboration, and delivering results that exceed expectations. Outside of work, I'm always learning—whether it's exploring new project management tools or mentoring young professionals entering the industry."

4. Experience Section: Go Beyond Job Titles

Your experience section should showcase more than just your job titles and dates of employment. Think of this as your chance to highlight the impact you've had in each role, not just the tasks you were responsible for. Each position should demonstrate the value you brought to the company.

Here's how to structure your experience section:

- Job Overview: A brief description of your role and responsibilities.
- Key Achievements: Quantify your accomplishments wherever possible. Did you save the company money? Increase revenue? Lead a team to success? This is what recruiters care about most.
- Impact Statements: Instead of listing tasks, focus on outcomes. For example, "Led a team of 10 engineers to deliver a critical project 2 weeks ahead of schedule, resulting in a £50k cost saving."
- Example:
- Senior Marketing Manager | XYZ Corp | January 2018 - Present
- Managed a £2M marketing budget, leading the development and execution of campaigns across digital, print, and social channels.
- Spearheaded a rebranding effort that increased brand awareness by 30% in 12 months.
- Implemented a new CRM system, improving customer retention by 15% and reducing acquisition costs by 10%.

5. Skills Section: Make Yourself Searchable

LinkedIn's algorithm relies heavily on the skills section when showing your profile to recruiters.

Most recruiters use skills filters to find candidates, so make sure your skills section reflects your actual expertise. Focus on adding relevant skills that align with the types of roles you're targeting.

- Prioritize Your Top Skills: LinkedIn allows you to pin three "top skills." Choose the ones that best reflect your personal brand and expertise.

- Endorsements: While endorsements aren't a huge factor in hiring decisions, they do lend credibility. Encourage colleagues and peers to endorse you for the skills that matter most in your industry.

6. Recommendations: Social Proof That Works

Recommendations are a powerful form of social proof. They're like mini-references directly on your profile and give recruiters an idea of what it's like to work with you.

Ask colleagues, managers, or clients to write you a recommendation highlighting specific strengths and contributions.

To make it easier for them, offer to write a draft or ask them to focus on particular areas where you excel.

7. Customize Your URL

One simple but often overlooked step is customizing your LinkedIn URL. Instead of a default URL with a long string of numbers, create a custom, professional link (e.g., linkedin.com/in/yourname).

This not only looks cleaner but is easier to share and helps with your personal branding.

8. Open to Opportunities: Let Recruiters Know

If you're actively looking for new roles, make sure you turn on LinkedIn's Open to Work feature.

This signals to recruiters that you're open to new opportunities without broadcasting it to everyone (you can restrict visibility to recruiters only). You can specify job titles, locations, and whether you're open to remote work.

Even if you're not actively job hunting, keeping the door open to recruiters can lead to conversations about roles that align perfectly with your career goals.

Your LinkedIn profile is a living document that should grow and evolve as you do. It's not just a resume—it's a platform for showcasing your expertise, sharing your insights, and building your professional network.

Keep your profile optimized, active, and reflective of your personal brand, and watch how opportunities come your way

CHAPTER 5:

MASTERING THE GIG ECONOMY & FREELANCE WORK

The gig economy has exploded in recent years, offering professionals a new way to work on their own terms. Whether you're freelancing full-time, taking on side projects, or considering a career shift into gig work, this chapter will help you navigate the ins and outs of freelance success.

Is Freelancing Right for You?

Before you dive headfirst into the gig economy, it's important to understand whether freelancing is the right path for you. While freelancing offers freedom and flexibility, it also comes with challenges—income instability, client management, and the lack of traditional benefits like healthcare or retirement plans.

Ask yourself:

- Do I value flexibility over stability? Freelancing offers control over your schedule, but there's also the uncertainty of inconsistent work.

- Am I self-motivated? Freelancers don't have bosses breathing down their necks. You're responsible for managing your time and delivering on projects without external pressure.

- Do I have a plan for slow months? Freelancing can be feast or famine. Some months may be full of work, while others are slow. Having a financial cushion or a backup plan is essential for long-term success.

Finding Clients

Finding clients is one of the biggest hurdles for new freelancers. Luckily, there are several strategies to land your first few gigs and build a steady stream of clients.

1. Tap Into Your Network
Your first clients are likely people you already know. Reach out to former colleagues, clients, or contacts who might need your services or can refer you to someone who does. Personal recommendations are powerful and can help you land gigs without relying on job boards or freelancing platforms.

2. Use Freelance Platforms
Freelance websites like Upwork, Fiverr, and Freelancer are popular starting points. While these platforms can be competitive and often drive prices down, they're a great way to build a portfolio and gain client reviews, which are valuable when you're starting out.

3. Optimize LinkedIn for Freelancing
We've already covered LinkedIn, but it's worth emphasizing that you can use it as a lead generation tool for freelance work too. Update your headline and summary to reflect your freelancing services.

For example:

"Freelance Graphic Designer | Specializing in Branding, Web Design, and UX/UI."

4. Build a Personal Website
A personal website or portfolio is essential for freelancers. It's where you can showcase your best work, testimonials, and services. Think of it as your digital storefront. Make it easy for potential clients to see what you do, how you can help them, and how to get in touch.

Setting Your Rates

One of the most challenging aspects of freelancing is figuring out how much to charge. Rates can vary dramatically depending on your industry, experience, and the type of clients you're targeting.

Here's how to set rates that reflect your value without underselling yourself.

1. Research Market Rates
Start by researching what freelancers in your field and experience level are charging. Freelancing platforms like Upwork have average rates for different industries, and you can also check job boards or talk to other freelancers.

2. Value Your Time
When setting your rates, consider how much time each project will take, including client communication, revisions, and any administrative work. You don't want to quote a price only to realize you've severely undercharged once the project is underway.

3. Charge by Project, Not Hour
Whenever possible, charge by project rather than by the hour. This helps you avoid situations where you're penalized for being efficient. It also gives clients a clear idea of the total cost upfront, making it easier for them to budget.

4. Be Ready to Negotiate
Clients may try to negotiate lower rates, especially if you're just starting out. Be prepared for this, but don't be afraid to stand firm.

If you offer a discount, make sure it's for a good reason (e.g., securing a long-term contract or working with a high-profile client who can bring you more exposure).

Managing Freelance Projects

Being a successful freelancer isn't just about landing gigs—it's about managing them effectively. You need to be organized, communicate clearly, and deliver high-quality work on time.

1. Set Clear Expectations
When starting a new project, be clear about what's included, deadlines, and any deliverables.

Miscommunication can lead to scope creep (when clients start asking for additional work that wasn't part of the original agreement), so get everything in writing.

2. Use Contracts
Even for smaller projects, always use a contract. It doesn't have to be complicated—a simple agreement outlining the scope of work, deadlines, and payment terms is enough to protect you and your client.

Tools like HelloSign or DocuSign make it easy to create and sign contracts digitally.

3. Stay Organized

Freelancing often means juggling multiple projects at once. Use tools like Trello, Asana, or Notion to keep track of tasks, deadlines, and client communications.

Being organized not only helps you stay on top of your work but also demonstrates professionalism to your clients.

4. Get Paid on Time

One of the downsides of freelancing is chasing down payments. To avoid this, make sure you agree on payment terms before starting a project.

For larger projects, ask for a deposit upfront—this protects you in case the client disappears halfway through. Also, consider using payment platforms like PayPal, Stripe, or TransferWise for secure and easy transactions.

Freelancing offers a world of flexibility, but it also comes with its own set of challenges.

Whether you're considering freelancing full-time or as a side hustle, success in the gig economy is about striking the right balance between finding clients, managing projects, and continuously refining your craft.

With the right approach, freelancing can open doors you never thought possible.

CHAPTER 6:
THE HIDDEN JOB MARKET

Most job seekers focus their efforts on job boards, company websites, and LinkedIn postings. But here's the thing: some of the best opportunities are never posted publicly.

This is what's known as the hidden job market—roles that are filled through word of mouth, internal hires, or recruiters reaching out directly to candidates.

Tapping into this hidden job market can give you a serious edge in your search.

Why Jobs Go Unadvertised

You might wonder why companies don't always advertise their openings. There are several reasons for this:

1. Confidentiality: Sometimes, companies need to fill roles quietly, such as when an employee is being replaced or a sensitive project is in the works. Posting the job publicly could raise red flags for the current employee or competitors.

2. Avoiding Overwhelming Responses: Posting a job online can result in hundreds (or even thousands) of applications, many of which are irrelevant. To avoid sifting through stacks of CVs, companies often rely on referrals or internal recommendations.

3. Internal Promotions: Before going external, companies often try to promote from within or ask employees for referrals. It's easier and cheaper to hire someone who already knows the company's culture and processes.

4. Recruiter Reliance: Many companies outsource their hiring to recruitment agencies or headhunters, who actively search for candidates without advertising the role.

Understanding why jobs stay hidden can help you position yourself to tap into this market.

How to Access the Hidden Job Market

1. Leverage Your Network
Your network is your gateway to the hidden job market. By consistently building and nurturing relationships, you'll increase the chances of hearing about job openings before they're publicly posted.

Here's how to make the most of your network:

- Reconnect with Old Contacts: Reach out to former colleagues, clients, or mentors. Let them know you're exploring new opportunities, but do so in a genuine way. Catch up first, and naturally lead the conversation toward your career goals.

- Stay Top of Mind: Even if you're not actively job hunting, keep your network warm. Share articles, comment on their LinkedIn posts, or check in periodically. When a hidden opportunity arises, they're more likely to think of you.

2. Work with Recruiters
Recruiters are often the gatekeepers to unadvertised roles, especially for senior or specialized positions.

Here's how to make the most of working with recruiters:

- Find the Right Recruiters: Look for recruiters who specialize in your industry or the types of roles you're interested in. Build relationships with them, so they keep you in mind when roles become available.

- Be Proactive: Don't just wait for recruiters to reach out to you. If you know a recruiter who works in your field, send them a brief message introducing yourself and your career goals. Be clear about the types of roles you're targeting.

3. Make Cold Outreach Work for You
Don't be afraid to approach companies directly, even if they're not advertising open roles. Many businesses are open to hiring talent, even when they're not actively recruiting.

Here's how to do it:

- Research Target Companies: Make a list of companies you'd love to work for, and do your research. Look for growth trends, recent news, or leadership changes—these can be signs that a company may need new talent soon.

- Find the Decision Makers: Instead of applying blindly, try to find the decision-makers in the department you want to work for. LinkedIn is great for this—look for department heads or hiring managers.

- Send a Personalized Message: Craft a brief but compelling message. Introduce yourself, explain why you admire the company, and highlight how your skills align with their needs. This shows initiative and can get you on their radar for future openings.

Example Cold Outreach Message:

"Hi [Hiring Manager], I've been following [Company Name] for a while and am particularly impressed with [recent project/news].

I'm a [your job title] with expertise in [relevant skills]. I'd love to explore any opportunities where I could bring value to your team.

Please let me know if you're open to a conversation."

4. Attend Industry Events and Conferences

Networking at industry events, conferences, or meetups is one of the best ways to access the hidden job market. Often, you'll meet people who know about openings before they're posted, or who can introduce you to decision-makers.

- Be Strategic: Don't just attend any event. Focus on industry-specific conferences or niche meetups where hiring managers or recruiters are likely to be present.

- Follow Up: After meeting someone, don't forget to follow up with a LinkedIn connection or an email. Mention something specific from your conversation and let them know you're open to future opportunities.

5. Build Your Personal Brand

The stronger your personal brand, the more likely you are to attract opportunities from the hidden job market.

If you've positioned yourself as a thought leader in your field, you may be approached for roles you didn't even know existed.

- **Publish Content:** Share your insights and expertise on LinkedIn, write blog posts, or give presentations at industry events. The more visible you are, the more likely people are to think of you when a role opens up.

- **Engage with Industry Leaders:** Comment on or share posts from thought leaders in your industry. This keeps you on the radar of influential people who may have access to unadvertised jobs.

The hidden job market is where some of the best opportunities lie—often out of sight from traditional job boards and postings.

By leveraging your network, working with recruiters, and proactively reaching out to companies, you can access roles that others might not even know exist.

With the right strategy, the hidden job market can be your ticket to finding a role that fits your goals perfectly.

CHAPTER 7:

WRITING YOUR CV FOR DIFFERENT STAGES AND INDUSTRIES

Writing a CV isn't as tricky as many so-called "gurus" make it out to be. But the truth is, one CV format doesn't fit all. Depending on where you are in your career and which industry you're targeting, you may need to tweak your approach.

In this chapter, we'll break down how to tailor your CV to different stages of your career and specific industries.

CV Basics: What Every CV Should Include

No matter your level of experience or industry, every CV should include these essentials:

- **Contact Information:** At the top, include your full name, email address, and phone number. You can also add a link to your LinkedIn profile and portfolio if relevant. Don't bother with your full home address—city and country are enough.

- **Professional Summary:** This is a short, 2-3 sentence overview of who you are, what you bring to the table, and what you're looking for. It should align with the role you're targeting.

    Example:

    "Experienced software engineer with over 7 years of expertise in full-stack development. Skilled in leading agile teams and delivering scalable solutions that improve business outcomes. Looking to bring my technical and leadership skills to a dynamic tech startup."

- **Skills:** Include a list of your key skills. Be specific, especially for technical roles. Rather than just listing "Project Management," specify the methodologies you're familiar with (e.g., Agile, Scrum).

- **Experience:** For each role, include the job title, company name, dates of employment, and key responsibilities. Focus on measurable achievements (increased revenue, reduced costs, improved processes, etc.).

- **Education:** List your highest degree first, followed by relevant certifications. If you're mid- to late-career, you don't need to include your graduation year unless it's recent.

Tailoring Your CV for Different Career Stages

1. Early Career (0-5 Years of Experience)

If you're just starting out, your CV should focus on showcasing your potential rather than extensive experience.

Employers know you're still building your career, so emphasize transferable skills, relevant coursework, internships, and any projects or volunteer work.

- **Highlight Internships and Projects:** If you've had internships, co-op placements, or worked on significant projects in school, these should take center stage on your CV. Even if your experience is limited, focus on how you contributed, what you learned, and the impact you made.

- **Skills Matter:** Since you might not have a long work history, emphasize your skills. Tailor this section to match the job description, but don't overstate what you can do—employers will ask about the skills you list.

    Example:
    - *Digital Marketing Intern | ABC Marketing Agency | Summer 2022*
    - *Assisted in the execution of digital campaigns, increasing website traffic by 15%.*
    - *Conducted SEO keyword research to improve blog performance.*

2. Mid-Career (5-15 Years of Experience)

At this stage, you should focus on your accomplishments, particularly how you've contributed to the success of your previous employers.

You want to show that you've not just been doing the job, but excelling at it.

- **Quantify Achievements:** Whenever possible, back up your claims with numbers. Instead of saying "responsible for sales growth," say "increased sales by 25% year-over-year."

- **Don't Dwell on Early Roles:** If you're 10+ years into your career, early jobs like internships or entry-level roles no longer need as much space. Instead, focus on the past 5-10 years where you've made the biggest impact.

    Example:
    o   Senior Sales Manager | XYZ Corporation | 2015 - Present
    o   Led a sales team of 15, consistently surpassing annual targets by 20%.
    o   Implemented a CRM system that reduced customer churn by 10%.
    o   Expanded client base by 30%, driving £5M in new revenue.

3. Late Career (15+ Years of Experience)

If you're more advanced in your career, you may want to consider a functional CV format that focuses on skills and expertise rather than listing every job chronologically.

Employers care less about your junior roles at this stage and more about the leadership and strategic value you bring.

- **Focus on Strategy and Leadership:** Your CV should showcase your ability to lead teams, drive business results, and implement strategic initiatives.

- **Condense Older Roles:** If you've held multiple roles over a long career, there's no need to include every single detail. Focus on the most recent and relevant roles. Earlier positions can be summarized in a "Previous Experience" section without listing out every responsibility.

    Example:
    o   Director of Operations | Global Enterprises | 2010 – Present
    o   Spearheaded company-wide process improvements that led to a 15% reduction in operational costs.
    o   Managed a team of 50 across multiple departments, improving team efficiency and morale.
    o   Directed the expansion of the company into three new international markets, increasing revenue by £10M.

Your CV is a dynamic document that should evolve as your career progresses. Whether you're early in your career, mid-level, or a seasoned professional, a well-tailored CV that highlights your unique skills and accomplishments is your key to standing out in any industry.

Customize it for every stage of your career and the specific role you're targeting to maximize your chances of landing an interview.

CHAPTER 8:
ADVANCED LINKEDIN TECHNIQUES

By now, you should already have a strong LinkedIn profile that reflects your career story and showcases your skills. But there's more to LinkedIn than just having a polished profile.

If you want to stand out, especially in a competitive job market, you need to take your LinkedIn game to the next level.

1. Use LinkedIn as a Content Platform
LinkedIn isn't just a digital resume—it's a content platform where you can build thought leadership, engage with industry trends, and showcase your knowledge. Here's how you can get started:

- **Write Articles:** LinkedIn's built-in publishing platform allows you to write long-form content directly on the site. Writing articles about industry trends, insights, or your professional experiences positions you as a thought leader.

- **Share Regular Updates:** You don't have to write full-blown articles to be active on LinkedIn. Share articles or blog posts from others, comment on relevant news, and offer your take on developments in your industry.

    Example Post:

    "I've been thinking about how remote work is reshaping company culture. It's not just about the flexibility anymore—businesses that want to succeed need to rethink how they engage teams virtually. Here's an article that dives into the future of hybrid work."

- **Engage with Others:** Don't just post and ghost. LinkedIn's algorithm rewards engagement. If you want your content to be seen by more people, you need to actively engage with your network by commenting, liking, and sharing posts.

2. Use LinkedIn Groups Strategically
LinkedIn Groups are an underrated feature for networking. Joining the right groups can give you access to industry-specific discussions,

job leads, and a chance to engage with potential employers or peers.

- **Find the Right Groups:** Focus on groups relevant to your industry, job role, or professional interests. Look for groups where decision-makers, recruiters, or thought leaders are active.

- **Engage in Discussions:** Once you've joined, be an active participant. Answer questions, provide insights, and engage in conversations. This positions you as an expert and gets your name in front of the right people.

3. Optimize Your LinkedIn SEO

Just like Google, LinkedIn has its own search engine. Recruiters often use LinkedIn's search function to find candidates, so you want to make sure your profile is optimized for search.

- **Use Keywords:** Think about the keywords recruiters might use to find someone with your skillset. These could be job titles, technical skills, or certifications. Make sure these keywords are sprinkled throughout your profile, especially in your headline, summary, and experience sections.

- **Customize Your Headline:** Many people miss this crucial step. Your job title may not be the best keyword for recruiters to find you. For example, if you're a "Digital Marketing Specialist," but most recruiters search for "SEO Specialist" or "Content Marketing Expert," tailor your headline to match the most searched terms.

4. Recommendations: Building Credibility

As mentioned in Chapter 4, LinkedIn recommendations are a powerful form of social proof.

But there's more to it than just collecting a handful of generic testimonials. You want recommendations that highlight specific accomplishments and strengths.

- **Give to Get:** One of the easiest ways to get recommendations is to write them for others. People are more likely to reciprocate when you give first. Focus on writing genuine recommendations for colleagues, managers, or clients you've worked closely with.

- **Ask for Specifics:** When you request a recommendation, don't just leave it open-ended. Ask the person to highlight particular achievements or skills that align with your personal brand and the roles you're targeting.

5. Connect with Recruiters
Recruiters are one of the most valuable resources on LinkedIn, especially if you're actively job searching.

There's an entire army of recruiters who use LinkedIn Recruiter to find candidates, but you don't need to wait for them to find you. Be proactive.

- **Search for Recruiters in Your Field**: Use LinkedIn's search function to find recruiters who specialize in your industry or the roles you're targeting. Connect with them and send a brief message introducing yourself and your career goals.

    Example Message:

    "Hi [Recruiter's Name], I came across your profile and saw that you specialize in placing [your job role]. I'm currently exploring new opportunities and would love to connect and hear about any roles you may have."

- **Stay Engaged:** Even if you're not actively looking for a job, maintaining relationships with recruiters is a smart move. Engage with their posts, share industry news, and stay on their radar for future opportunities.

LinkedIn is far more than a job-hunting tool—it's a platform where you can build your personal brand, engage with thought leaders, and expand your influence in your industry.

By using LinkedIn strategically, from optimizing your profile to actively engaging in conversations, you'll open doors to opportunities that align with your career goals and expertise.

CHAPTER 9:

PREPARING FOR EVERY TYPE OF INTERVIEW

Preparing for a job interview can feel like an overwhelming process, but the more you prepare, the more confident and relaxed you'll be when it's time to sit down with the interviewer.

In this chapter, we'll cover how to prepare for every type of interview, from standard one-on-one interviews to technical interviews and even panel interviews.

1. The Basics: Research and Preparation
Every interview, no matter the format, requires some basic preparation. You should never go into an interview without doing the following:

- **Know the Job Description Inside and Out:** Re-read the job description carefully and think about how your skills and experience align with the requirements.

    Be prepared to discuss specific examples from your past roles that demonstrate you can handle the responsibilities.

- **Research the Company:** Go beyond the "About Us" page on the company's website. Look for recent news, check out their social media presence, and read employee reviews on Glassdoor.

    This research will help you tailor your answers to the company's values and goals.

- **Prepare Questions:** Asking thoughtful questions not only shows that you've done your homework, but it also gives you valuable insights into the role and company culture.

    Avoid asking about salary or benefits until the offer stage. Instead, ask about the company's goals, team dynamics, and success metrics for the role.

Example Questions:

- o "What do you enjoy most about working here?"
- o "How do you measure success in this role after the first 6 months?
- o "Can you tell me more about the team I'll be working with?"

2. Behavioural Interviews: Mastering the STAR Method

Behavioural interviews focus on how you've handled situations in the past as an indicator of how you'll perform in the future. The **STAR** method (Situation, Task, Action, Result) is a structured way to answer these questions.

Here's how it works:

- **Situation:** Describe the context of the situation you were in.

- **Task:** Explain the challenge or task you needed to accomplish.

- **Action:** Discuss the actions you took to address the task.

- **Result:** Share the outcome of your actions, including any measurable impact (e.g., increased sales, improved customer satisfaction).

Example:

Question: "Tell me about a time you had to lead a team through a difficult project."

Answer: "At my previous company, we had a critical software project that was falling behind schedule (Situation).

As the project lead, I was responsible for getting the team back on track (Task).

I organized a series of daily stand-up meetings, re-prioritized tasks, and communicated regularly with stakeholders to manage expectations (Action).

As a result, we were able to complete the project two weeks ahead of the new deadline and under budget (Result)."

3. Technical Interviews: Showcasing Your Skills

If you're applying for a technical role, you'll likely face a technical interview. This could involve solving coding problems, performing technical tests, or discussing specific tools and methodologies.

- **Brush Up on Fundamentals:** Make sure you're comfortable with the basics of your field. For software engineers, this might mean practicing algorithms and data structures. For designers, it could be reviewing design principles and best practices.

- **Work Through Problems Out Loud:** During technical interviews, it's important to explain your thought process as you work through problems. Even if you don't arrive at the perfect solution, demonstrating how you think critically and solve problems can impress interviewers.

4. Panel Interviews: Navigating Multiple Interviewers

Panel interviews can feel intimidating, but they're just like regular interviews with a few extra people in the room. The key is to stay calm, make eye contact with everyone, and involve each interviewer in the conversation.

- **Prepare for a Variety of Questions:** Since panel interviews often involve people from different departments, you may get a mix of questions. Some will focus on your technical abilities, while others may ask about how you fit with the company culture or how you handle teamwork.

- **Engage with Each Interviewer:** When answering questions, try to engage all the interviewers. Even if one person asks the question, make eye contact with everyone, and occasionally direct your answers toward different members of the panel.

5. Video Interviews: The New Normal

Video interviews have become a standard part of the interview process, especially for remote roles.

While they're similar to in-person interviews, there are a few additional factors to keep in mind:

- **Test Your Technology:** Make sure your internet connection is stable, your microphone works, and your camera is positioned at a good angle. You don't want technical difficulties to distract from your performance.

- **Dress the Part:** Even though you're interviewing from home, you should still dress professionally. Make sure your background is clean and free of distractions, and avoid any potential interruptions (e.g., pets, kids, noisy neighbours).

Interviews can be intimidating, but with preparation and the right mindset, they become an opportunity to showcase your skills, experience, and fit for the role.

Whether you're preparing for a one-on-one interview, a technical test, or a panel discussion, approach each interview with confidence and curiosity.

Remember: the interview is as much for you as it is for them.

CHAPTER 10:

SALARY NEGOTIATION MASTERCLASS

Getting a job offer is a great feeling, but before you sign on the dotted line, there's often room for negotiation. Salary negotiation is a delicate balance—you want to get paid what you're worth without risking the offer.

In this chapter, we'll cover how to approach salary negotiations confidently and effectively.

1. Do Your Research

Before you even step into a negotiation, you need to know your worth. Use resources like Glassdoor, Payscale, or LinkedIn Salary to research the salary range for your role, industry, and location.

Look at the Full Package: Compensation isn't just about salary. Consider the full benefits package, including bonuses, stock options, health insurance, retirement plans, and other perks. Sometimes a slightly lower salary can be offset by generous benefits.

2. Timing is Key

The best time to negotiate salary is after you've received a job offer but before you've accepted it. At this point, the employer has already decided they want you, and you have more leverage to negotiate.

Don't Bring It Up Too Early: Avoid discussing salary in the early stages of the interview process. If asked about your salary expectations, try to defer the conversation by saying you'd prefer to discuss compensation once you've learned more about the role.

3. How to Frame the Conversation

Negotiation doesn't have to be adversarial. Approach the conversation as a collaborative effort to find a solution that works for both you and the employer.

Highlight Your Value: Instead of simply asking for more money, explain why you're worth it. Reference specific skills, experience, or achievements that justify a higher salary.

4. Be Ready for Pushback

Employers may push back on your request, and that's okay. Be prepared to compromise, but also know your bottom line—what's the minimum salary or benefits you're willing to accept?

If the employer can't meet your salary expectations, consider asking for other benefits, like flexible work arrangements, additional vacation time, or professional development opportunities.

5. Practice Makes Perfect

Negotiating salary can feel uncomfortable, especially if you're not used to it. Practice the conversation with a friend, mentor, or even in front of a mirror. The more you rehearse, the more confident you'll feel during the actual negotiation.

Negotiating your salary is one of the most critical conversations you'll have during the hiring process. With the right preparation, a clear understanding of your value, and the confidence to ask for what you deserve, you can secure a compensation package that reflects your skills and experience.

Remember, negotiation is not about winning or losing—it's about finding a mutually beneficial agreement that sets you up for success in your new role.

CHAPTER 11:

AFTER THE OFFER—NAVIGATING YOUR FIRST 90 DAYS

The hard work doesn't end when you accept a job offer. In fact, your first 90 days at a new job are critical for setting yourself up for long-term success.

In this chapter, we'll cover how to make a great first impression, build strong relationships with your new team, and hit the ground running in your new role.

Build Relationships Early

The first few weeks in a new job are all about building relationships. Take the time to get to know your new colleagues, especially the key players in your department and the people you'll be working with closely.

Set Up One-on-Ones: Don't wait for your manager to introduce you to the team. Be proactive and set up one-on-one meetings with your new coworkers. Use these meetings to learn about their roles, how they prefer to communicate, and how you can best collaborate with them.

Learn the Company Culture

Every company has its own culture, and fitting in means more than just doing the job. Pay attention to how things are done—whether it's how decisions are made, how meetings are run, or how people interact with one another.

Ask Questions: Don't be afraid to ask questions about the company's processes, expectations, and goals. Showing curiosity and a willingness to learn will make a positive impression on your new team.

Set Clear Goals

Your first 90 days are about proving that you were the right hire, so it's important to set clear, achievable goals. Work with your manager to define what success looks like in the short term and what you can accomplish within the first three months.

Your first 90 days in a new job are your chance to make a strong impression, build relationships, and set the tone for your future success.

By taking a proactive approach, learning the company culture, and establishing clear goals with your manager, you'll not only prove that you were the right hire—you'll set the foundation for long-term career growth within the company.

CHAPTER 12:
CAREER GROWTH AND DEVELOPMENT

Once you've landed the job, the focus shifts from searching to growing. Career development is about more than just showing up every day—it's about building a long-term strategy for advancement, skill acquisition, and personal fulfilment.

In this chapter, we'll explore how to continue growing in your career, position yourself for promotions, and stay relevant in an ever-changing job market.

Take Ownership of Your Career Path

Many people make the mistake of waiting for their employer to steer their career progression. While your company might offer development programs or promotion opportunities, it's ultimately up to you to chart your own course.

- **Set Long-Term Goals:** Where do you see yourself in 5, 10, or 15 years? Your goals don't have to be perfectly clear, but having a sense of direction helps guide your daily decisions. Do you want to move into leadership? Specialize in a specific area? Transition to a different industry?

- **Regular Self-Assessments:** Take stock of where you are and where you want to go. Review your performance every six months—not just in terms of the tasks you've completed, but in how you've grown professionally. Are you building the skills needed for your next role?

Skill Building: Stay Relevant

One of the fastest ways to stagnate in your career is to stop learning. In today's fast-paced world, the skills you have today might not be the ones you need tomorrow.

- **Identify Skills Gaps:** Look at your industry and the roles you're targeting next. What skills are required that you don't have yet? This could be technical skills, leadership abilities, or industry knowledge.

- **Continuous Learning:** Enroll in courses, attend workshops, or earn certifications. Platforms like Coursera, Udemy, and LinkedIn Learning make it easier than ever to learn new skills on your own time.

    Not only does this make you more valuable in your current role, but it also makes you more competitive when it's time to move up or move on.

Find a Mentor or Sponsor

Mentorship is one of the most effective ways to accelerate your career growth. A mentor provides guidance, shares insights, and helps you navigate challenges.

But for real career advancement, you might also need a sponsor—someone who actively advocates for you in rooms you aren't in.

- **Finding a Mentor:** Look for someone in your company or industry who's a few steps ahead of where you want to be. Don't be afraid to reach out and ask for advice or mentorship. Most people are flattered and happy to help.

- **What is a Sponsor?:** While a mentor gives you advice, a sponsor goes a step further by actively opening doors for you. They might recommend you for a promotion, introduce you to key people, or help you secure a high-visibility project.

    These relationships often develop organically, but you can also proactively build them by delivering consistently high-quality work and aligning yourself with influential leaders.

Stay Visible

As you grow in your career, visibility becomes increasingly important. It's not enough to do great work—people need to know you're doing great work. This means being proactive about highlighting your achievements.

- **Share Your Wins:** Regularly update your manager on your accomplishments. If you've achieved significant milestones or contributed to major projects, don't assume people will automatically notice—tell them.

- **Public Speaking and Thought Leadership:** Look for opportunities to speak at industry conferences, write articles, or contribute to panels. Being known as a thought leader in your field can lead to more career opportunities, whether it's promotions, consulting work, or even headhunting offers.

Career development is an ongoing process, and it's up to you to take the reins. Whether you're seeking promotions, expanding your skill set, or positioning yourself as a thought leader, your growth journey is about continuously evolving.

With the right mindset, mentorship, and learning opportunities, you can shape your career to align with your long-term vision.

CHAPTER 13:

CAREER PIVOTS & RETURNING TO WORK AFTER A BREAK

Changing careers or re-entering the workforce after an extended break can feel like starting from scratch.

Whether you're looking to pivot into a new field or return after a break for parenting, caregiving, or health reasons, this chapter covers how to make a smooth transition.

1. Making a Career Pivot

Switching to a new industry or role can seem daunting, but with the right strategy, it's completely doable. The key is positioning your transferable skills and bridging the gap between your current experience and the job you want.

Identify Transferable Skills
Look at your current role and industry. Which skills are universally applicable? These might include project management, leadership, communication, or technical skills that carry over into different fields. Highlight these in your CV and LinkedIn profile.

Reframe Your Experience
Your work history might not align perfectly with your new career goals, but you can reframe it to emphasize relevant skills and experiences. For example, if you're moving from marketing to HR, highlight your communication and people management skills.

Bridge the Gap
If your new career requires technical knowledge or skills you don't have yet, find ways to bridge the gap. This might mean taking a few courses, earning certifications, or volunteering for projects that allow you to build the necessary skills.

2. Returning to Work After a Break

Whether you've been out of the workforce for a few months or several years, re-entering can be challenging. The key is to own your career gap while demonstrating that you've kept your skills sharp and are ready to contribute immediately.

Be Honest and Confident
There's no need to hide or downplay a career break. Be upfront about why you took time off, whether it was for caregiving, illness, travel, or personal development.

Frame the break positively—highlight what you learned, how you stayed engaged with your field, or the soft skills you developed (e.g., time management, problem-solving).

Show You're Ready to Re-Enter
Employers want to know that you're ready to jump back in, so demonstrate that you've kept your skills up to date. Mention any relevant courses, certifications, volunteer work, or freelance projects you've done during your break.

Network Your Way Back
Networking is critical when returning to work after a break. Reach out to your old colleagues, mentors, and industry contacts to let them know you're back on the market.

Attend industry events or join LinkedIn groups to reconnect with your professional community.

A career pivot or return to work after a break is not a step backward—it's an opportunity to reinvent yourself and pursue new challenges.

By emphasizing your transferable skills, staying confident in your abilities, and networking with intention, you'll find that the next chapter of your career can be just as fulfilling, if not more, than the last.

CHAPTER 14:

NAVIGATING TOXIC WORK ENVIRONMENTS & KNOWING WHEN TO LEAVE

Dealing with a toxic work environment can take a serious toll on your mental and emotional well-being.

Whether it's a micromanaging boss, toxic coworkers, or an unhealthy company culture, this chapter will help you recognize the signs of a bad workplace and decide when it's time to move on.

1. Recognizing a Toxic Work Environment

Toxic workplaces can manifest in different ways, but common signs include:

- **Micromanagement:** If your boss constantly hovers over you, second-guesses every decision, or refuses to let you work independently, this can create a stressful environment.

- **High Turnover:** If people are constantly leaving the company or department, it's usually a sign that something is wrong.

- **Lack of Transparency:** If your company is secretive about decisions, financial health, or promotions, it can create an environment of distrust.

- **Bullying or Disrespect:** A toxic workplace may include disrespectful behavior, cliques, gossiping, or outright bullying. If your workplace is filled with negativity, it's a serious red flag.

2. Coping Strategies for Surviving a Toxic Workplace

If you're not in a position to leave right away, there are ways to manage the situation while you plan your exit.

- **Set Boundaries:** Toxic bosses or coworkers often take advantage of those who don't set clear boundaries. Be firm about your limits when it comes to workload, overtime, and personal time.

- **Document Everything:** Keep a record of any incidents of harassment, bullying, or unreasonable demands. If things escalate, this documentation can be valuable for HR or legal proceedings.

- **Find Support:** Seek support outside of work—whether it's through friends, family, or even professional therapy. Having a network to lean on can help you manage the stress.

3. Knowing When It's Time to Leave

Sometimes, the best option is to walk away. If your job is damaging your mental health, your work-life balance is nonexistent, or you've stopped growing professionally, it might be time to leave.

- **Assess the Damage:** Take a hard look at how the job is affecting your well-being. Are you constantly stressed or anxious? Are you dreading going to work every day? These are signs that the damage might be too much to recover from while staying in the role.

- **Plan Your Exit:** Before you quit, make sure you have a plan. Start your job search while you're still employed, if possible, and line up a new opportunity before giving your notice.

Toxic work environments can wear you down, but you have the power to choose what's best for your mental and professional well-being.

Whether you decide to stay and set boundaries or make the difficult decision to leave, remember that your health and career growth should always come first. Knowing when to walk away is a strength, not a weakness.

CHAPTER 15:
JOB SEARCHING IN A GLOBAL MARKET

The rise of remote work and global teams has opened up job opportunities across borders. In this chapter, we'll cover how to navigate the global job market, whether you're looking for remote work, planning to relocate, or seeking roles in multinational companies.

1. Remote Work: Expanding Your Options

Remote work allows you to apply for jobs regardless of location. This can dramatically expand your job search options, but it also means you're competing with a global pool of candidates.

Here's how to stand out in a remote job search:

- **Highlight Remote Work Skills:** Working remotely requires certain soft skills, like time management, self-discipline, and communication. Make sure these are front and center in your CV and interviews.

- **Research Time Zones:** When applying for remote roles, consider the time zone differences. Some companies may require you to work within certain hours, while others are more flexible.

2. Relocating for Work

If you're considering moving to a new country for a job, there are additional factors to consider:

- **Work Visas**: Research the visa requirements for the country you're targeting. Some companies may sponsor your visa, but others might expect you to handle it yourself.

- **Cost of Living:** Make sure the salary being offered

matches the cost of living in the new location. A great salary in one country might not go as far in another with a higher cost of living.

3. Tailoring Your CV for Global Markets

Different countries have different expectations when it comes to CV formats and content. In some countries, including a photo or personal information (like your marital status) is common, while in others, it's discouraged.

- **Research Local Norms:** Before applying to international jobs, research the local CV format and expectations.

    For example, in many European countries, it's customary to include a photo on your CV, while in the U.S., this could raise concerns about discrimination.

The global job market offers exciting opportunities, but it also brings new challenges in terms of competition and logistics.

Whether you're applying for remote work or considering relocation, stay adaptable, research thoroughly, and tailor your approach to the specific demands of the international workforce.

With the right strategy, your next job could be anywhere in the world.

FINAL THOUGHTS: YOUR CAREER, YOUR JOURNEY

Job searching is hard work, but it's also a chance to reflect, grow, and take control of your career. By following the strategies outlined in this book—from writing a killer CV to mastering interviews and negotiating your salary—you'll be well-equipped to tackle your next job search with confidence.

Remember: This is your career, and no one will care about it more than you. Take ownership, keep learning, and never be afraid to ask for what you're worth.

Good luck out there!

Free Resources, my blog and social channels

www.ingramcontent.com/pod-product-compliance
Lightning Source LLC
Chambersburg PA
CBHW070421230526
45471CB00006B/2913